THE SIMULTANEOUS DRESS

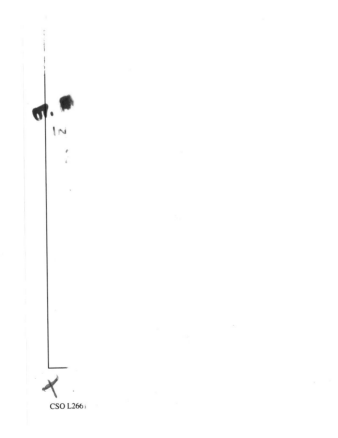

Books by Linda France

Red (Bloodaxe Books, 1992)
Sixty Women Poets (Bloodaxe Books, 1993)
Acknowledged Land (Northumberland County Council, 1994)
The Gentleness of the Very Tall (Bloodaxe Books, 1994)
Storyville (Bloodaxe Books, 1997)
The Simultaneous Dress (Bloodaxe Books, 2002)

LINDA FRANCE

THE
Simultaneous
Dress

BLODAXE BOOKS

ISBN: 1 85224 573 5

First published 2002 by
Bloodaxe Books Ltd,
Highgreen,
Tarset,
Northumberland NE48 1RP.

www.bloodaxebooks.com
For further information about Bloodaxe titles
please visit our website or write to
the above address for a catalogue.

Bloodaxe Books Ltd acknowledges
the financial assistance of Northern Arts.

Cover printing by J. Thomson Colour Printers Ltd, Glasgow.

Printed in Great Britain by
Cromwell Press Ltd, Trowbridge, Wiltshire.

for Subhadassi

Acknowledgements

Acknowledgements are due to the editors of the following publications in which some of these poems first appeared: *Frank's Casket, Golden Girl* (Credo Press, 2001), *The North, The Rialto, Smoke, Tabla Book of Verse 2001* and *Star Trek: The Poems* (Iron Press, 2000). 'St Cecilia' was commissioned for Hexham Abbey Festival 1999 and 'Homage to My Latin Teacher' for Writing on the Wall 2002, an international writing project based along Hadrian's Wall.

Contents

There is no cure for hot and cold.
There is no cure for the facts of life.

CHÖGYAM TRUNGPA RINPOCHE

Naked

Nobody tells you this is what it's like
growing older: every day as if you were
being born all over again. Again and again.
Raw, unfledged. The way you have to work
it all out from scratch and still not settle
on a convincing answer. All you know is
you're naked – stark, belly, buff –
a little bit softer, a little bit colder;
the air lifting the hairs on your skin
as near as you'll get to wherever it is
you're going, the way it is the way
it is. More than a wanton unbuttoning,
the shell of your skin's split open. Nothing
as clear as outside and inside, as good
or bad: all one big simultaneous song
and all the people singing it as naked as you are.

The Woman Who Wore Her House Like a Dress

Every morning she would begin again:
a mannequin – new season, new colours.
She'd feel rooms like robes stroking her skin
as she sashayed through – powdery paint
or smudged metallic, dusty blue wool.
Her watered silk curtains clocked with gold
were a disguise designed to match her eyes.
Her stairs were Schiaparelli, rippling
and dangerous...

From outside all you could see was old stone
frilled at the edges, flashes of glass
like cheap jewels. Crossing the threshold
was undoing the zip at the back
of a fitted shift, long and black. It let you in.
And then the walls would tumble around her
in shivers of plush and almost-naked
so her breath was silver and no one saw
the cobwebs...

Better that way than when nothing fitted
and she tore at it, lamenting in French
so many deaths, the time she remembered
when women were women and wore their houses
like ball gowns, ruched and gorgeous,
pillars of satin and lace, history
that catwalked and kissed the air, smelling
of Chanel – 5, 19, *Allure* –
the colour of money...

More and more she played Cinderella
in her kitchen, wisps of torn chiffon,
tap-water chic, a curtain ring chilly
on her third finger. She held herself up
to the light to test the kindness of colours,
the fit of slippers. She would watch herself
in all her shining mirrors – her puzzled face,
white and moony; a single sequin,
her eye for style...

Corrections

I take a red pen to my life, cross out
words like daughter, mother, wife;
strike out all those oughts and buts,
the endless hopeful lies. Every day
it's getting shorter. Even vanity fades
along with bloom and giggle and slender.
Last thing to go is my mind, never mine
anyway. Like everything else, a story
to keep myself uptight and occupied,
on the right side of my demon teachers.
Each page is a horror of blots,
omissions and errors. I hear myself
thinking Could Try Harder. Try to
ignore it, harder and harder; not to
set my heart on ticks and stars, on how
it might feel to be recycled,
a clean sheet of paper, a fresh draft;
someone else's name at the end.

Not a Dress Rehearsal

Flesh

Looking in the sea's rippling mirror,
I caught the grace of my own shadow;
feet the wrong shape underwater, fat
and fleshy, taking root in the sand squelched
between my toes. I was a sea tree: salt water
to cool me; sun to lift me higher; gulls screaming
in the bleached cathedral of my ears.
I raised towers, scoured moats, planted
paper flags with dragons on, lions roaring.
Always in my own skin, the burn of it
beneath blue nylon, sand peppering the rim
of my thighs. I knew the limits of it,
the scratch of pleasure, the horizon's stretch.

Paper

The sun sank. Winter came to rest on my shoulders,
a good coat, room to grow. My world turning
into words, black and white, I was happy to be
a cut-out *Bunty* doll, an outfit for every occasion.
I'd sleep in a shoe-box while a witch called Singer
stitched me dresses out of fabulous scraps
from window displays, cowboy tents, curtains. One,
in fuchsia felt, zipped right up to my chin, made me feel
like Emma Peel. If someone had given me a pair
of knee-high boots, I would have gone up in flames.

Blood

Still pink, those shrill weekends, I learned
to dance in a v-neck shift with darts
and seams; shades of rosebud, carnation
my sister had sewn for me, as if she knew
what was blooming beneath the brimming
Berlei A-cup. She made a hat to match
I hardly ever wore, not knowing what shape
my face should make under its dipping brim.
There were five Lindas in my class. I claimed
the distinction of a moon shining above my *i*.
Went halves with my best friend on the first issue
of *Cosmopolitan* – a double-page spread of a nude
whose name was Paul. We didn't know a man
could look that strange without his clothes on.

Feather

The same best friend I shared everything with,
even the letters of my name, a Chelsea Girl,
with dreams to spare, gave me one: long, chiffon,
black as crows' wings, all the shadows I'd ever shed.
I wore it when I felt like flashing my loveliest eyes
at men from Dorset or Persia, who smelled
of smoke and Aramis. I felt high as a bird, tall
as the past. That was when I first tasted
champagne, resolved never to take no for an answer.
And all my clothes happened to me like accidents.

Camouflage

I swooped through Oxfam shop and jumble sale
into a world where nothing but my skin fitted.
I smothered myself in smocks, moth-eaten fur.
I wanted to wear the red books I was reading,
battledress; girded my loins against invasion.
Funny, how my skin swelled into a cloud, mushrooming
my belly; its spores spinning a child out of air
and purple and vodka, a dream I'd had of his name.
Flesh turned inside out and I was naked.

Milk

I moved in and out of my body like a ghost.
My breasts were clocks, chiming the hours
of my babies' little bird mouths. I was a game
of cards, head, torso, legs in different squares,
wearing different clothes. Dresses and sex
were against the rules. As soon as I could,
I broke them. I thought I'd get my body back
but it galloped off at the first scent of fox.
I missed my birds. An empty dress, second-hand
and stained; that smell clinging to its folds,
the milky whisper of their warm breath.

Bone

In the dredge of chlorine, the glare
of the full-length mirror at the baths,
I check the inventory of lost and found –
the drifting shape I make when I walk;
the heat I feel under my skin, that stray
accent of desire; the anxious aches of age
and gravity, distance. I count the years,
a prize I don't know if I deserve; test
the strength of muscle, the amnesia of flesh.
Let this nakedness be enough, my best dress.

The Call of the Night

(after the painting by Paul Delvaux)

If I didn't know better I'd think my hair
had turned into a fall of ivy.
Its weight tilts my head back so my chin
is the chin of a proud and superior
woman. I want to walk barefoot and visit
my friends, the ghosts of trees. It's only
a small thing – this idling and leafy nakedness –
but it says a lot: the way I think of you
as mountains on the horizon
with a better view of the sky. The way
I miss you when you're not there, the rattle
and blue of you. The way my eyes are not my own.
Light is filtering into the monochrome
and skin's skin-coloured, earth's compost and loam,
and my hair, down to the ground, is green.

The Lady's Mantle Letter

She will write him a letter to tell him
   how cool and wet her garden is this July,
     how beautiful the alchemilla is,
       a strange citrus, petal-less froth above
         the green nearly-circles of the fanned leaves.

They are the shape of its other name –
   Lady's Mantle – an outspread cloak, pleats
     stitched with pearls of dew, scallop-edged;
       designed for wrapping and unwrapping,
         a honey-scented aphrodisiac.

'Alchemilla' is after 'alchemy' –
   the magic water it breathes through its leaves
     part of the ancient recipe for melting
       metals into gold. She will tell him
         what waiting is and what it isn't.

She will write him a letter to tell him
   these things because she's feeling inside out
     and he's not there to unwrap her, wrap her
       in his pashmina arms; and because
         it's him she's thinking about when, by chance,

she places three stems of purple crane's bill
   in the same vase and catches the shock
     of both flowers growing more alive,
       their colours spilling into something new.
         She will tell him how soft the rain is.

Love
(after Anna Akhmatova)

Sometimes it coils like a snake,
spitting its spells about the heart.

Sometimes for days on end it coos
like a dove through an open window.

Sometimes it sparkles in the frost;
gleaned in the surrender of wallflowers...

But its unmarked roads will always
lead you away from home.

It knows the guile of the violin,
songs like tears, like prayers.

And there's the terror of catching it
in a smile that will always be strange.

Ghazal of Unexpected Love

(after Lorca)

No one could fathom the fragrance
of your body's dark magnolia.
No one guessed you martyred
love's hummingbird between your teeth.

A thousand Persian ponies dozed
on your brow, its moonlight plaza,
while for four nights I reined
that enemy of snow, your waist.

Between walls and jasmine, your glance
was a bleached bough of seeds.
I looked in my heart to give you
those ivory letters that spell *always,*

always, always: my garden of suffering –
you're forever slipping through my fingers;
your life's blood on my lips,
and your lips, already bleeding for my death.

Ghazal of the City in Winter

The city is walking through winter.
All the scattered lights are flowers
blooming through razors, blue, blue sky,
brushstrokes of acetone clouds.

Stone is spellbound and cappuccino
on the Quayside. And even though
it's the darkest month and this black
and white city doesn't know whether

to hold back or let go, I surrender
to the turquoise arc of the bridges,
this gypsy I'm kissing under one of them,
counting the sixes of his pink paisley scarf.

I stand on tiptoe to reach his lips,
breach the fallen roar of the Metro,
the slow river at our side. I print the ace
of desire on his skin, my scarlet petals.

Constellations

(after the series of paintings by Joan Miró)

> *Although there will be scars and plenty of them, it is good*
> *to remember that in tensile strength and ability to absorb*
> *pressure, a scar is stronger than skin.*
>
> CLARISSA PINKOLA ESTES
> Women Who Run with the Wolves

The light through the window can't decide
if it wants to be pink or blue, misted

with our exhalations, a plain at dawn,
making itself new. Time and the world

dilute us, distill us, drop by drop.
We look into each other's eyes

as if we'll find something we lost
so long ago we can't remember what

it is. You sing the history of your walls –
flamenco, copper, full fathom blue,

two coats of yellow – and offer me
the most expensive date in Africa

before peeling off my clothes so slowly
I hardly notice. Until I'm naked

and floating in a pool of lilac,
breathing hard through my mouth the way I do

when I'm so very there I stop thinking.
I hitch a ride on the heron's legs

around your eyes and where we go is just
the beginning.

*

The moon is lying on its side like your smile
in the morning when our eyes open
at the same time.
              Small town lights are a swarm
of bees, honey gold and tambourine.
                              Somewhere
over the rooftops the click of castanets
stings my heels into hooves.
                    Under a halo
of the deepest blue, we toss pesetas
in the wishing well; listen to its round mouth
suck on our dreams and swallow the stones.

I tie a white shell called tenderness
on a silk thread around your neck.
                              You tell me
I'm a bell and I'm dazzled by the shine
of myself, ringing and ringing.

*

Once I saw two horses, one brown,
one black, dancing in a field.
I want us to dance like that,
not touching, you in your purple shirt,
me in my new suede shoes, lifting
our chins and laughing in Spanish.

*

Your teeth marks on my thigh are one constellation.
Another, in the sky above the road
to the city, I'll call *The Hands*.
                            I'm scared
they'll come and get me. I'm scared they'll leave me
alone.
        I know they're my father's hands,
their faded sepia, their fragrance
of tobacco and mustard.
                            I pull them down
to earth so I can hold them, stroke the blisters
of their broken promises.
                        The promises
your hands make are easier to keep –
ice-cream spiced with ginger; a clementine
plucked straight from the tree; your inky blue
messages lit up like manuscripts,
the lick of your ys and ampersands
like kisses with rucksacks, the first letter
of your name, a heart.
                        Your eyes trace the flight
of my hands, measure how much air they need.

I'm trying to imagine the night sky
emptying itself of stars, the sadness
of a life without those fingertips of light,
their give and take, their gentleness.

*

Take this pear.
Feel the chill
of its tight skin
against your lips.
Bite it. Taste
the white flood
on your tongue.

*

There is a scald on my right calf the shape
of an island we visited like birds
in winter. Eight freckles hovering
beyond its northern shore are two of them,
beaks open wide with singing; how we kiss
and taste each other's air.

Now the clocks in our bellies are wound so tight
we think this sprinkled pinch of sun is spring.
I wear my coat like a long shadow.
In the castle of its dark I remember
that summer I lost my pony tail.

I'd cry for that little girl, the grit of sand
between her toes, if I couldn't see how big
the world is, the way its crazy paving
from this high up is patched with sadness.
You remind me I'm still here; touch my hair
as if it were your own.

You're growing on me like a second skin,
the sweet fleece of you warming my cold bones,
that fist in my shoulder. We make a feast
of each other in the soft bowl of my bed.
All we need more of is time, the best knives
that cut clean and glitter.

Freckle Face

Summer teatimes my father read the stories
in my face. He'd make an inventory
of every sunny day's crop of freckles
until there weren't enough numbers to match
my splashy browns, the sting of my blushing pink.

Stroking her children's freckleless faces,
Mrs James told me they were stains, a sign
my mother left me outside in the rain
when I was a baby. Back at home Dad said
they showed I was beautiful. And I glowed.

After so many winters they're relaxing
into ruddy, unfreckling themselves
in a rash of wrinkle and pore. I peer
into the mirror, trying to scry
the late-night scribble of their story.

My face wears dot-to-dot constellations
of what I've lost – a tightness I'm glad
to be rid of – and what I've earned – a new world
of valleys, contours I mapped myself.
I raise the flag of it, content with wayward lines.

Rose Tattoo

Worker's hands. Gold watch.
Soldier's rose tattoo. Through a forest
of thorns I explored the pulse of it,
the pink petals of it, his half-seas-over
Queen and Country rose, fragrant
with factories, sweat and tobacco.

His sturdy skin and my good gardening
kept it blooming, the perfect curl of it,
the hidden treasure of it. And the shrapnel
seeding his back, the stretched pores.
My father's body was my history book.
It taught me about work and wars and sadness.

When he died, the little girl in me
cried her heart out for it, for Daddy,
for England, that last tattoo, her lost rose.

Connoisseur

My father was a connoisseur
of women's bodies but even after
their first few dates he failed
to notice the difference between
rolled-up stockings and my mother's breasts.
He'd watch films on Saturday afternoons
starring Gina Lollobrigida
and Sophia Loren. My father admired
women like that – full-breasted,
full-lipped, Latin-tempered, Latin-eyed –
the exact opposite of my mother, a woman
nearly as invisible as her breasts.

One who lived down our street
he christened The Shape, fascinated
by the ballast of her square bosom,
her ample swaying behind: the way
they tipped her off-balance when she walked.

Another he waltzed with a little too close
my mother hated. She'd pretend not to see her
if they were both on the same bus home
while I gawped at the gold in her ears,
the mink at her throat, the black-pencilled
beauty spot on her pan-sticked face,
trying my father's shoes on for size.

Easter

Every year you'd knit us all
new jumpers; send them in the post,
sleeves filled with shiny chocolate eggs.

This year I'm craving something soft,
in blue, a colour I never wear.
Your eyes following me around.

Compass

Tonight it's just the two of us
drifting on the raft of evening.
You are upstairs drawing a leaf

you went outside in the soft dark
to pick, wearing my old green shoes
that have grown too small for you.

I'm sitting at the kitchen table
nursing the ache in my left breast
with malt, thinking about family.

How it's just a broken mirror.
How you make your own luck.
How you can't count your chickens.

Before you were born I wrote
your name in a book and you came true
like a wish – your father's eyes, my lips.

There is no map for what we're making.
Just the shape of a single leaf,
its five-pointed compass, open as air.

Any Mother's Son

You say all you want is to have some fun.
Your bloodshot eyes are raw but they still shine.
Baby, you could be any mother's son.

You can't even remember what you've done.
It's all a fog of vodka and cheap wine.
You say all you want is to have some fun.

The clock's a thin black bird at nearly one.
Even though I know it's you and you're mine,
Baby, you could be any mother's son.

When they take your picture I want to run.
They tell you to sign on the dotted line.
You say all you want is to have some fun.

They write *Tattoos, distinguishing marks: none.*
Magistrate's Court, Newcastle upon Tyne.
Baby, you could be any mother's son.

If it's manhood's colours you think you've won,
Why should it be me who pays the fine?
You say all you want is to have some fun.
Baby, you could be any mother's son.

The House With No Doors

If this were a dream, you'd understand it
better – if you'd come home from a hot place,

your skin rare and fragile as burnt coral,
to a house with no doors, an Escher sketch,

somebody's idea of a joke; to Janus
squatting on every threshold, sticking out

his two tongues, the mad arrows of his eyes –
all his gate-keeper's laws of in and out

broken, no rhetoric to match this brazen
free-fall yawn. Every room melted into

one room, even the stairs are going nowhere,
open-plan. The pitch of it isn't cricket –

nothing to whisper behind, to cover
your lies, your nakedness. No brass apples

to cider your palm. No click behind you
like the silence around the sound of your name.

All the colours collide and crash. All your screws
are loose. Packets and cans fly off the shelves

in the pantry onto your bed. The bath
is full of aspidistra and clockwork clowns.

Even the dog loses her nose for smells
spilling out beyond their compass – woodsmoke

and rose, garlic and toothpaste. Your house
is half-finished, undone, no longer home.

The wind has sucked away all its sweetness.
You can't translate this word you know is *empty*

but see it in the ghosts of children's shoes,
the blunt morse code of the droppings of mice.

When is a door not a door? When it's a jar
of air, unhinged and gaping, a keening mouth.

Or the cave of your body, the trembling
ventricles of your inconsolable heart.

See how you've grown so used to *this is this*
and *that is that*, you can't live with *just so*,

the implacable flow of the one
and the same. *Enough*. Let all the doors

which aren't there be open. Let the key be
your breath as you watch it furnish your only room.

Homage to My Latin Teacher

(for Mrs Stanley Hall)

You swept into the lesson, dressed in red,
chalk dust powdering your hair, your patrician nose,
already translating Parkstone Grammar
First Form into AD 43:
our first taste of your noble, passionate tongue.

Salvete puellae! And we'd chant back
Salve domina! The exclamation mark
a chorus of chairs scraping the tiled floor
as we sat, a fizzing cohort of girls.

You rolled the words around your mouth and sucked
the juice out of them. I hid at the back
and watched you spit. Like a mother bird,
you fed us from your own lips – *the table*;
to the table; *by, with, from the table.*

And so I learnt to unravel the puzzle
of the 'Unseen', marvel at the precision
of syntax and rhetoric, recognise
the English in the squares of the mosaic.

We could all have cheered at Cicero's coaxing,
wept when Dido flung herself on the pyre,
but knew that someone had to found Rome
or else we'd have no baths, no straight roads,
no alphabet from which to build our own.

Your daughter was in the year above mine.
I wondered how it would be to have you
as a mother; if you talked Latin at home.

Talk Time

Isn't the voice an erogenous zone?
The way lips, teeth, tongue tease air into sound.
That's how I feel when we talk on the phone.

I listen to him laugh, whisper and moan,
tell me what it's like to be verbed and nouned,
agree the voice is an erogenous zone.

He makes me growl like a dog with a bone,
drool and pant and wag. I'm his faithful hound.
That's how I feel when we talk on the phone.

There's nothing better when you're on your own.
His words down the wires wrap me round and round.
Hear it. The voice. An erogenous zone.

His is like ice-cream and I'm the cone.
We melt together, one hot sticky mound.
That's how I feel when we talk on the phone.

It might begin with the dialling tone
but where we'll go is breath-, sweat- and bed-bound
because his voice is an erogenous zone
and that's how I feel when we talk on the phone.

Klingon Sestina

It is among the Klingons that love poetry achieves its fullest flower.
LIEUTENANT WORF

There isn't much I don't know about love.
It's a point of honour for a Klingon –
to go beyond the final frontier;
to be open and fearless, the Captain
and the crew of their starship passions. Space
is a place for loving: do it boldly.

Fall in love boldly so you'll write boldly.
You can't have one without the other. Love
is a white-hot black hole in outer space;
light is fast and lonely. Whisper Klingon
galactic sweet talk and, like our Captain,
you'll never fail to cross the frontier.

A lot's been said about that frontier,
a lot of jokes about going boldly.
But you've got to admit Kirk and Captain
Picard – neither of them went short on love.
We taught them all they knew of the Klingon
arts of desire, singing sonnets in space.

To write poems you need plenty of space.
Every line is a new frontier
of pain. And it's true, lovers can cling on,
anxious and craving. Just tell them boldly
how many moons you must orbit for love
of their phaser thighs. Show them who's Captain.

That's one of life's ironies our Captain
understands: the more you love, the less space
you have; not worlds enough or time to love
forever; no cosmos, no frontier
far enough to hold it all. Compose boldly
in your own tongue. I'll read it in Klingon.

There's something about the sound of Klingon
that drives all sane beings wild; the Captain
included I must confess. *Go boldly*,
Jean-Luc is all I need to say. Then space
ripples between us and no frontier
remains. We're one on our planet of love.

I am the Captain of couplets in space.
Let me boldly erase this frontier,
my love, your clothes. Trust me, I'm a Klingon.

Sonia Delaunay Visits the Bigg Market

(after Blaise Cendrars)

Where does a woman's body end
and her dress begin?
Her body is irrepressible,
radiant as truth is
but here her clothes are all stitched up
with little white lies, designed
not by artists but therapists,
pimps, conjurors, crooks.
My eyes are tired of this
window shopping, this junk couture.

As night slips off the coathanger
of the sky, all a woman's curves
whirl and spin. She's taking
her clothes out but where
does her body begin?

The colour of sun-bed skin is tough,
inedible, a leather vessel
for pouring drink in, zipped shut
with the vacuum twist of her navel.

The city's paved with women's navels,
smiling or sucked in, wrapped
around metal, viscose, adrenalin.

The chemical colours of a woman's body
come out to play –

the Big Macs of her breasts
Slumberland belly
the Super 8 of her arse
neon smile.

The city's a catwalk
for her and her tigers,
heels tapping out minutes
as they pass like sewing machines,
the fidget of silver needles, the purr.

The woman wears her sleeves out
with holding on. Her arms
are bare. The cut of her frock
is sharp as her tongue.

After midnight the pavement
is all pizza and sequins,
thin rivers of broken dreams.

On her hip the woman keeps
the secret of a tattoo, dangerous,
blue, as if she regrets the edge
of her skin, the bridge
of her broken body.

Sonia Delaunay Listens to Miles Davis

Jazz happens
where there was none
like paint, circles
and half-circles, path
of a dark snake,
side-winding a halo,
shining the kind
of blue that swims
through sadness,
small squares – tall
buildings waiting to fall
under the weight of sky.

Someone's laughing
in black and white,
shrugging in flashing lights.
Cars cruise in the rain,
chequered taxis taking
corners like oaths.
The city's dancing
in syncopated shoes, red
leather, yellow leather.
Steam breathes
off tarmac, curves
stretching into nothing,
the ghost of a voice.

The sun will rise.
It will be midnight.

Billie Holiday at Carnegie Hall

Her fingers mistook her hair
for a thought they had once
and let go and kept letting go
until the pin sunk into skin
tight on her scalp. Everyone

knows how much heads bleed.
Billie's black dress hid the stains.
Her three gardenias pouted,
white against the darkening red.
On stage, she held up her head

like she always did and sang
and kept on singing until the smell
had died the same way day falls
into night; its ghost cradling her,
that sweet motherish scent.

The Love Song of the New Driver

Let us drive then, you and I,
On those roads that rise with us to meet the sky
Like an Irishman lifting a glass of Guinness;
Let us drive, through the frosty sodium town,
The smooth, sober route down
Past unlit windows and monochrome stones,
The illegible litter of traffic cones:
A town that wants to be what it once was, and now
Is not – where it seems a cow
Can pose a mad, unanswerable question:
Oh, do not ask, *Where to now?*
Let us drive and start our journey.

In the car the driver grips and steers
Thinking of her different gears.

The faceted headlights spill their jewels in the driver's eyes,
The faceted frost sparks its glamour in the driver's eyes.
Against the soft black, they both mirror the bright stars
That catch and guide the thin lilt of her sighs;
Wheel her gently along the fat curve of roundabouts;
The late lostness enough to make her weep;
And seeing that it is a cold December night,
Wrap themselves around the car and fake sleep.

And let's say: isn't now the time
For the faceted frost that jewels the streets
Spic-sparking its glamour in the driver's eyes;
This is the time, this is the time
To look, listen and match the gear to the turn of the wheel.
There is a time to burn, to accelerate,
And time just to wait, to coast in neutral,
To be prepared for the five-bar gate.
Time for cars and time for men,
And there's always time for the Highway Code,
Time for thinking and braking, that other road,
Before the taking of four-star or oil.

In the car the driver grips and steers
Thinking of her different gears.

And let's say: isn't now the time
To reckon *Should I speed?* and *Should I speed?*
Time to gauge the snaking incline's need,
The hoped-for protection of St Christopher's beads.
But they say *She's new. See, her L is green.*
At junctions she stalls; what she signals isn't what she means.
She works hard at it, tries and tries; knows it's not enough to be keen.
(So who was it who advised: *See and be seen?*)
Should I speed
Down this stretch of tarmac?
Behind the wheel, all I can do
Is remember tomorrow, guide my hatchback along the switchback.

For I have been up and down this road before –
I have sensed how the adverse camber runs,
I have measured the miles in shoe leather, thumbs;
I know how the engines roar
Out of the slinking invisible roads.
    So what is this Highway Code?

And I have known these red and white lights before –
Those lights that catch you, vulnerable in their glare,
And when I was vulnerable, spooked as a rabbit,
My ears twitching in rusty semaphore,
Who taught me the habit
Of understanding spares and repairs?
    Who taught me the Highway Code?

And I have known those hot and sour fumes before –
Fumes that curl toxic in your nose and throat
(Fumes for which there is no known anecdote).
Is it freedom of the road
That makes me write this ode?

Carbon monoxide that makes a person cough, retch or choke.
So why should I write odes?
    Is it just a habit?

.   .   .   .   .

Should I say, I have floated on the edge of roads
After dark, like a moth drunk with headlights
Burnt to a white cinder by their heat and dazzle?

I should have been a pair of angel's wings
Fluttering above the scenes of accidents.

.   .   .   .   .

And the tarmaced carriageways, roads stretch so gracefully!
Planned by men in rooms,
Careless of death…or me…or fumes,
Scribbled across the land for you and me.
This concern for internal combustion,
Will it result in redemption or extinction?
And even though I've abstained, prevaricated,
Even though I now know the snarling pressure of the car behind,
I stand – and drive – alone, can't speak for mankind;
I have seen from both sides the way the cold wheels grind,
And I have witnessed the failed start, the sad demise of the Big End.
I am implicated.

So I ask is it worth it, after all?
After all the questioning of your skills,
How to deal with junctions, reversing, rust in your sills?
Is it worth it to have
The chance to step into a car and halve
The time of your journey, time enough to ask
Yourself all those other important questions?
Will I be able to find a place to park?
Am I a member of the RAC? –
While others say, competent, unafraid,
The ones who say *Just look: this is the task,*
The ineluctable task.
Looking back, is it worth it after all,
Worth the grief, the expense,
After the carefully catalogued timetables,
After the recording of arrivals and departures and the missed
        connections,
Remembered with affection –
What am I now – the driver or the driven?

I am both, courting disaster, thrilled to be uncrowned king of
      the road.
Is it worth it to have
The keys to the kingdom, a shining second-hand car.
And clicking in the safety belt I'll say: *Car,*
    Show me the way to go.
    This is the way to somewhere else.

      .   .   .   .   .

    Yes! I *am* Graham Hill, and I *do* have a beard;
I'm a person who knows what a wheel
Can do, twists and turns, trusts the rubber keel,
How three hundred and sixty degrees can rule.
Responsible, calculating risks,
Aware, cautious, but ready to go;
At times, something akin to soaring.
At times a self-propelled fool.

    I drive slow...I drive slow.
I run the heart of my carburettor low.
Shall I grease my nipples so? Does my throaty exhaust leak?
The mechanic, in his oily overalls, takes a peek
And discovers what makes my engine shriek.
I have heard it from behind the wheel, roaring
Its song, thirsty for oil, petrol and love,
As we all are, hungry for food and love.

We all have eyes to locate the road ahead,
To follow the lights, carry our licence,
To steer ourselves towards significance.

Cooking with Blood

Last night I dreamt of Delia Smith again –
smoked buckling simmering on the horizon,
that old Doverhouse moon stuffing the dumpling
of a crackling sky. She played en papillote

for just long enough to sweat me garlicky.
After I'd peppered her liver, stuffed her goose
and dogfished her tender loins, she was paté
in my hands. She got all mulligatawny

so I tossed her into a nine herb salad
of Hintlesham. She was my Russian herring,
my giblet stock. We danced the ossobuco;
her belly kedgeree, her breasts prosciutto.

I tongue-casseroled her ear she was my Queen
of Puddings and wouldn't we sausage lots
of little quichelets, a platter of sprats
we'd name Béarnaise, Mortadella, Bara brith.

But when the trout hit the tabasco, it turned out
she was only pissaladière, garam
masala as a savoyard. Arrowroot.
Just another dip in love with crudités.

And I've stroganoffed with too many of them.
I chopped home to my own bloater paste and triped
myself into a carcass. No wonder I woke up
with scarlet farts, dried blood under my fingernails,

dreaming of Delia, her oxtail, again.

The Old Convent at West Ogwell

If you were the eye of God, what you'd see
is a key unlocking the green rising
above the church tower. In the year
of our Lord 1954, concrete
was glory and fishpond and plane tree
and the Sisters of the Community
of Jesus the Good Shepherd considered
the lilies of the field and toiled with spades,
crucifixes tapping against handles
as they bent, wide sleeves cuffed, wellingtons
juicy with good earth, good rain. Roof slates
and footpaths are shiny as snakes; trees hiss,
swaying like waves. Everyone says it's wet
in this part of the world. Inside
worn floors – marble, slate, scrubbed linoleum
that will never come clean – keep the code
of small footsteps measuring the space
between chapel and kitchen and upstairs
to the single room I'm sleeping in now,
flung, hoydenish, on the narrow bed.
I'll get up to the ghost of a bell
and open thin curtains timidly-crimsonned;
watch the metal-framed window
for signs of light, signs the rain might stop
long enough to invite shadows across
the threshold like visitors, bringing news
of another world: the way the nuns let
the gift of chocolate melt on their tongues
after all that silent chewing of glamourless food;
everything cooked beige to match the walls.
In a corner of the churchyard, south-easterly,
the sisters are buried in unmarked graves.
If you were a vessel of God, the rain would fall
would fall through you, body and soul, rinse you clean.

St Cecilia

I *St Cecilia and the Doves*

Like warm milk, the sounds of morning spill
through her window, sunshine splashing her face.
The doves on the rooftops sing the city awake.
Their wings lift her hands in prayer.

In the space behind her eyes she sees nothing
but white; the whole world a swathe
of billowing linen, swaddling clothes and shrouds.
Her mother has taken to weeping.

She insists the blind see deeper, farther;
hear the mysteries of the invisible,
whispered blessings, the roar of glory.
A wafer of feathers melts on her tongue.

II *St Cecilia Sets Sail*

On the night of her wedding she plays
with an angel; the rhythm of her breath
a song from the heart, a shell at her ear.
Her elbows kindle the crackle of silk,

hoist a sail plucking the strings of the wind.
If anyone cared to look what they'd see
is a small woman dressed in white, sitting
very still, more nun than bride; her staring eyes.

All she wants is that hush where she can hear
the sigh of the sea, its rolling refrain;
can weigh the treasure stowed in the hold
of her angel boat, her salty anchor.

III *St Cecilia Dances in the Rain*

She is a circle of light, unwinding
a reel of rain from her spinning centre.
Her belly's a crescendo of diamonds;
her body a glass, both empty and full,

like a horn, coaxed by lip and tongue
to glisten into more than hollow brass.
She can't tell where she ends and the rain begins.
This is the beauty of being here and now,

the bliss in and under the skin and bones.
She is a woman who dances naked in the rain,
trusts the rhythms of air and water;
each step a cross, kissing the thirsty earth.

IV *St Cecilia Rows Home*

The coda is the creak of a gate
swinging open, a carillon of bells,
the sweet smell of Sicilian roses,
the soft surrender of their white petals.

The cloth tightens on her face when they try
to suck her air to stone. She thinks of feathers.
Just behind her ears the sword is a storm.
She keeps on breathing and thinks of oars.

For three days she counts the city sounds,
those bells, angels singing. And something else
she'd only caught in whispers before,
the bravura flourish of all God's colours.

Tantala

She's not standing up to her neck in water
but every single day she's taunted by desire.
The small delights that make a life worth living
are there for the wanting, for the taking.
For the paying. They tell her she's worth it.

The sons and daughters of desire are desire.
Who's saying *Stop*? She wants it all. She wants more
and more. Who mentioned greed? The next thing
she buys, eats or drinks, the next person she meets
will make her happy, make everything All Right.

Even though she does it to forget, escape,
it's a wheel that doesn't fit. She's fed up
and hungry. On and on, the whisper of wanting,
that guilty itch. She's not standing up to her neck
in water but, watch her, she's drowning.

Fresh. Open. Hot.

You can't weigh me with feathers or books.
You can't count me with clocks.
I am thin as a spy in the house of desire.
I change with the weather, play the dominoes
of night and day. What I have to say
is silence. I listen to the birds singing,
watch the polka of their wings. My hair
is the colour of the wind when it's not there.
I am a chemistry lesson on what happens
to fire when I breathe in. My hands will touch you
like a whisper you can't quite catch. You'll fall
through me and notice how very small the world is,
how much you'd miss me if I went away.

A Manual for Living by Water

The Pebble Trick

We've even started dreaming about boats,
the sound of the sea salting our lips
as we breathe. By day we test the accident
of 'tamarisk', 'sea urchin', 'fig'.
The church bell is a white song in a white bed
on a soft evening made for nothing but this –
letting everything blow away
in the wind, holding everything
by the hand like a friend. That's what I wish for,
glimpsing it on the horizon, an island
we can visit, stay as long as we like.
You say you want to be a pebble
on the beach or a bird eating the blue
of the sky. Behind my turquoise eyes
you're already there. I can see you flying,
your back glinting in the sunlight like wet stone.

Mirror

You come inside me like a sea horse
as the shell of me opens and I cry.

The sea brings me back to life, catching me
in its net of diamond shadows.

When I said you'd never let yourself
be loved, I was talking about myself

My throat is full of stones; your face
more familiar than my own. I will be

a tamarisk tree and thrive on salt water;
feel the breeze ruffle my firework feathers,

my fishbone leaves, lift them like the hairs
on my arms when you look at me that way –

as if I were made of sea glass set in gold.

A Rumour of Pearls

When the blue hour comes between day
and evening, the light empties itself
across my breasts. My cuttlefish heart
is made of paper, crackled at the edges;
its secrets spiced with sand, a rumour
of pearls. I trace a single word in gold –
                    Threshold
– a necklace of doors to keep on opening.

Earth Like Iron

Out of the shade of the juniper tree
the cloudless sky higher than the hillside
is a blue door we must walk through to sift
the dust of the deserted village.

Empty houses surrender their stones
to the sun. The old roads have lost
their memories; their tumbling away
the only nothing that happens.

Someone read a newspaper here
in 1974. He listened to the transistor radio
and kept bees. His cupboards smell
of red earth and naphtha.

What ghosts there are keep their silence;
crows black fruit spiked on prickly pears.
What words there are burnt into ochre –
over and over and over.

Hunger

His body has ripened
into the dark honey of dried figs.
I peel him from the stalk
and split him open,
taste the sweetness of his seeds.

The Old Ones

Although it's not the custom
I want to touch their faces,
the roasted sesame of them,
their weathered walnut,
the shapes of their curiosity,
indifference, wisdom.

I want to tell the stories
in their eyes, salty and dark
as olives, always looking out
to sea, waiting for the ferry
they'll never catch, done with
all that fuss and hunger.

Mica

Out in the day everything had just been born.
I was emptied out of myself into myself,
hollow as the cave, as the bell I rang
when we left, iron against iron –
sturdy, triumphant – the muscles
in my thighs – a dream of lightness.

Driftwood

He asks me what shape the sea is.
I tell him it looks like the world,
that part where we don't live,
something we know better
from outside like our own bodies.

I think he is asking me something else –
the enormous why of speaking
and listening, the current
of how we live together.

I tell him it is potent and lemony,
a bed of glass, shushing
in tune with the barracuda moon.
 And driftwood is what's left
when the sea is gone,
bleached, broken and full of worms.
It is the sea's wounds;
rust like blood in the sand.

Stagshaw Dhamma

Somewhere in Thailand a golden statue
of David Beckham kicking the air, hair
keeping the secret of his eyes, is set
before the temple Buddha. The monks
don't know his name but the Abbot says
football is religion to millions and the truth,
if you look, is everywhere.
                              In a field
in the North of England I am looking
at the everywhere all around me.
The land is high and wide, so many shades
of green. It is one with the weather
and what we call time but is really the truth
telling itself over and over and us
listening to it,
                      hanging on the edge
of the golden light and the earth rising
up to meet it and the sheep who are eating it,
black faces chewing, fat hearts beating
beneath the floating highway of pylons,
the sky-soaked purr of a plane sailing past
the wideopen eye of a brimming moon.

The End of August

The pink hollyhocks announce themselves
to the valley. The lower blooms are waving
their creased dark flags. The tight buds
right at the top will never open.

For twenty miles square there's no stock.
Only a single dog, barking for the collie on heat
over the fell. And the hollyhocks
at the window, smelling of nothing, swaying.

The Sleep of Butterflies

The night the war started
she came back from the city
smelling of smoke. All her sentences
stopped too soon; and the wind
buffetting the house wouldn't.
She needed a bath to wash it off,
repeating to herself: *the world is*
like this, for just this minute, like this.

All will be well.

In the crease between wall
and ceiling two butterflies roost
in a sleep they may never wake from;
hold on tight as if they know
there will be another summer,
even though their wings are torn,
losing the dust of their colours.
More like fragments of a lost mosaic
than butterflies; from the bath
she can't tell if they're admirals or peacocks,

what manner of things will be well.

*

And in the morning another one
in the bedroom is tricked awake
by her breath warming night air.
It flies around the room, nowhere
to rest – a garden that's too white –
wings ticking very fast.

She doesn't know what is best,
what is right – leave it alone
or open the window and let it out
into the weather, getting colder
every day, too cold for butterflies
already bruised and out of season.

The fear in its wings is the beat
of her refugee heart.
She watches it tire and hide
inside the big white flower
of the lamp. Somewhere to let
the darkness come, the light:
the same way we try to forget
there's nowhere on earth to go.

*

If she hung herself up
in a corner would all be well;
folded her wings in on themselves,
never forgetting there is no forever,
would all manner of things be well?

After some brave blue-gold days
and a hard night's frost,
the dark runes of the butterflies
are all erased. The dream
is broken. In her white flag
of a house she'll pass the winter
alone and sleepless.

Trying to Explain Telescope

(for Andrew Waterhouse, 1958–2001)

Telescope. A device for looking
at the world from a distance.
If you were from the moon
I'd just been watching through one,
the magnificent, unfathomable mirror
of its lens – open-mouthed at curves,
halo, pockmarks, its surface pitted
as pumice and close as my own heels –
if that was where you came from,
where we must assume there are no
telescopes, I'd show you one. Here:
the shiny black cylinder, hard
and scientific; the way it collapses
into itself, becoming smaller, blind
and of no use. I'd demonstrate how
you can lift it, open, to your eye
and look at the stars, their late blaze,
their conjuring of swan and horse
and fog. You would discover more
shapes, other functions. We might share
what we both know is cracked laughter.
How can I not let you keep it
in your hands, a gift to mark
our meeting, our almost total
lack of comprehension?

Globe

The white chrysanthemum is a small world
in water, the blue air of my new vase.
Its globe of many petals shines, crying
'Live well together for you are alone.'

I would like to be that wise, that fresh: blessed.
But every day the other world, the one
my feet rest upon, tells me something else,
a tale about forgetting, restlessness.

The dense, tender bloom won't fit in my hand.
I stroke it like a newborn baby's head,
with a mother's love, a gardener's trust,
the tips of my fingers remembering.

Bodhisattva

See how her eyes are like gulls, gliding
across the white mist of her face.
Or whales swimming in the deep of it.
So liquid is her skin, her hair hesitates
to begin. Her nose studies the curled petals
of her tiny lips and decides to name
everything *lotus* and *flush* and *open*.

What can you do with a woman like that
but lay your head in her lap and breathe
the heat from her belly, the *in*, the *out* of it?
Bring her the courage of your sadness
because that's all you have left and let
the calm weight of her hand soothe you,
her total absence of drama and façade.

The map around your sternum you try to keep fixed
she melts, matching you breath for breath.
You are molten gold, older than angel hair.
You've lost all your edges. Which one
of you lifts up her head? Borrow her crown,
those flames. Your neck will be a column of air.
Wish all the people wisdom, wish them well.

The Simultaneous Dress

The trick with a simultaneous dress
    is that you wear it *underneath* your skin
and let it show through, like a fancy vest
    under net. What you get is what you think.

You needn't go shopping for tailor-made
    or off-the-peg as you can't try it on
and then take it off. It's just there – the grace
    of breath. Call it *alive*. Love it or not.

It isn't what's known as wearing your heart
    on your sleeve: your *bones* remember your dreams
and they change the world around you. Your last
    days won't be spent twitching every seam and crease.

    All you really own is the light it holds
    in its endless, simultaneous folds.